HISTORY OF THE AMERICAN ESKIMO DOG

WHAT'S IN A NAME?

We hear that you cannot always tell a book by its cover, and that sentiment certainly holds true for the American Eskimo. Hearing this dog's name, one is likely to envision a large, athletic wolf-like dog with dark eyes, a thick coat of hair, and a bushy tail that curves up over the animal's back, harnessed to a sled that it gregariously pulls across the frozen tundra. Meeting this dog in person, however, will instantly shatter all those expectations.

Contrary to its name that conjures up images straight from Alaska and the world of Jack London, the American Eskimo is not a sled dog. With its largest representatives standing no taller than 19 inches at the shoulder,

The elegant, sweet-natured American Eskimo Dog defies expectations: it is neither truly American nor a native sled puller of the Arctic.

and most of its kind standing much shorter than that, a team of Eskies would be hard pressed to meet the challenge of pulling a sled through Arctic snow.

Another source of confusion in the American Eskimo's name is the fact that this dog is not American—not at its roots, that is. The Eskie, as it is known to its friends, is the descendant of an illustrious family of dogs that is represented throughout the world in a variety of breeds of all names, colors and uses. While it boasts the word "American" in its name, the Eskie's roots span back much further than those of the so-called New World to a time when America was not yet even a concept, let alone a discovered land.

Despite its rather misleading name, the Eskie is blessed with a rich heritage of which it may be quite proud, and it occupies an important niche within the households of those humans it calls its own. While this niche does not involve sleds and tundra trails, it is nevertheless an important one that has forever been intertwined with our own.

marked by a thick double coat, a pointed muzzle, erect ears and a lush, thickly furred tail that in some breeds curves up over the back. These dogs are also renowned for their attachment to humans. Though typically independent in their thinking, they are old souls that bond deeply to their people and often seem able even to read their minds.

A northern breed related to the Samoyed and the other Spitz breeds, the American Eskimo Dog represents the classic Arctic dog type: double coat, pointed ears and muzzle, and a well-furred tail that curls over the back.

AN ANCIENT PAST

Within the canine family tree, there is a branch occupied by a group of dogs known as the northern breeds. Though they differ in color, size, work and geographical home, they all bear a striking resemblance to one another.

The greatest similarity is in the dogs' appearances, as each is

Such attachments are often the products of an ancient past, and this is indeed true of the northern breeds of dogs. The family includes, among others, the Samoyed, the Alaskan Malamute and, of course, the American Eskimo. Estimated to have lived with humans as established canine types for at least 6,000 years, and perhaps longer, the northern breeds are presumed to be some of the very oldest domestic dogs.

This estimate is more than a guess, as images of wolf-like dogs with curled tails in decidedly affectionate poses with humans appear in carvings and similar artistic renderings from ancient archeological diggings and historical archives all over the world. It would appear that smiling dogs of this type were fixtures in ancient Greece, Rome, the Middle East, the Arctic and Europe.

Throughout their long history, the mutual affection between the northern dog breeds and the people in their lives has been immortalized in art, literature and personal accounts. Owned by such luminaries as King George III and his wife Queen Charlotte, Wolfgang Amadeus Mozart, Queen Victoria and Franklin Delano Roosevelt, the breeds' attachment to the human species has crossed all geographic and economic boundaries.

It is the European branch of this very democratic family, specifically the German branch, that would beget the dog we now know as the American Eskimo. Germany boasts a proud tradition of canine husbandry, one of those revolving around the so-called "Spitz" dogs, Germany's homegrown members of the northern breed family.

It all began with the German Spitz, a dog of decidedly northern characteristics that was immensely popular in Germany in the 1600s and 1700s. Unlike so

Beloved of royalty and the common folk alike, the American Eskimo comes to owners today with an impressive, ancient past.

many of the northern breeds—the sled dogs in particular—that are known as poor watchdogs, the German Spitz was renowned for its incorruptible inclination to protect its home and family. It was most often called to this duty by working people in rural and urban areas alike, happily installed in homes, boats, fields and wagons to keep intruders at bay.

It is the northern breeds' democratic attachment to humans that propelled the earliest stages of the development of the American Eskimo in the 1800s. During this time, a great many Germans migrated to the United States, and many of them,

Unlike the German Spitz breeds from which the American Eskimo no doubt derives, the American breed can only be seen in solid white. The German breeds can be any color or combination of colors.

not surprisingly, brought their German Spitzes, with them. In time, these dogs would become America's own special contribution to the world's Spitz, or northern breeds. That contribution would be the American Eskimo.

THE TWENTIETH CENTURY ESKIE

Today it is not at all unusual to walk down the street with an American Eskimo by your side, encounter someone of German descent, and be complimented on your lovely "Spitz" that so reminds this individual of his or her childhood in Germany.

Despite the long history of small, white Spitz dogs as companions to human families,

the twentieth century is credited with solidifying the American Eskimo as we know it today. Within this century it has gained increased popularity as a pet (which can have both positive and negative effects on a breed), stardom as a circus and movie dog, with its athletic agility and quick, trainable mind and featured heavily in advertisements, in America and abroad.

Yet despite the American Eskimo's multi-faceted popularity and its increased recognition on streets, in the media and in the show rings of America, the twentieth century has also presented some obstacles to this sprightly German native. The century's first world war spawned a great deal of anti-German sentiments, both in America and in Europe. Given the deep emotions such sentiments touched, they affected all areas of culture, including the canine aspects of culture. This then, is why the lively white Spitz would become known as the American Eskimo.

In the early years of the twentieth century, the name "Spitz" was instantly recognizable, even to those with no interest in or knowledge of dogs, as a word of German extraction. As American soldiers fought the Germans overseas, the dogs native to that nation would naturally become symbols of that opponent. Thus, as German Shepherds in Britain would become known as Alsatians, enthusiasts of the white Spitz dogs in America would begin seeking a change in the name of the object of their passions as well.

In 1913, the American Eskimo was granted recognition as a breed by the United Kennel Club, recognized as the Spitz or American Spitz. Aside from the after the kennel name of one of its pioneering twentieth century breeders.

Although German immigrants would (and still often do) continue to call the dog a Spitz, its new name began taking hold throughout the 1920s and 1930s, when its following experienced a

These three tikes are German Zwerg Spitzen, the smallest of the five German Spitz breeds. They resemble the Pomeranian but are in fact more ancient. In size, the Mittel Spitz resembles the Miniature American Eskimo and the Giant Spitz, the Standard.

anti-German response the name could elicit, the name was far too generic in a world populated by a plethora of so-called Spitz breeds. A new name was in order. The breed was christened the American Eskimo, not in honor of an ancient career as a sled dog or life in the Arctic among the Eskimos, but rather, it is told, similar and very enthusiastic surge. So beautiful a dog is not easily forgotten when spotted walking along a busy city street or quiet suburban sidewalk. While many who encounter this dog assume that it must simply be a miniature Samoyed, those who take the time to learn more find out this is not the case at all.

Yet despite its breathtaking beauty, it has taken the Eskie several decades to receive full traditional public recognition as a breed. Frankly, that is how many enthusiasts have preferred it. As a UKC breed, it has enjoyed its career in the UKC show ring and the relative anonymity that has helped it land in homes with people who know how to handle its exuberance, vitality, and independent nature. The breed has enjoyed its own special brand of popularity, recognized and admired primarily as a pet and companion, with a strong word-of-mouth following as the primary advertising vehicle behind it.

This situation is in the process of changing, however. For the majority of this century, the Eskie was sometime show dog, full-time family companion—not a bad role for a dog. The 1980s and 90s, however, have witnessed a profound increase in the breed's visibility and recognition, one that culminated in 1994 when the American Eskimo was recognized by the American Kennel Club.

The UKC recognizes two American Eskimo types. The "standard" male Eskie stands over 15 inches to 19 inches at the shoulder, while the female stands over 14 inches to 18 inches. The "miniature" male stands 12 to 15 inches at the shoulder, females 11 to 14 inches. The AKC recognizes the standard American Eskimo (over 15 inches to 19 inches at the shoulder) and the miniature (over 12 inches to 15 inches at the shoulder), but it also recognizes the "toy" Eskie, which stands 9 inches to 12 inches at the shoulder. Regardless of size, however, all Eskies should sport a white double coat, erect ears, a lush tail that curls up over the back, dark eyes and black points (nose, lips and eye rims).

Now seen in both the UKC and AKC show rings, the American Eskimo's visibility to the public at large promises to increase tremendously in the years to come, a phenomenon that longtime enthusiasts both relish and dread. Few can resist the charm and beauty of the American Eskimo, yet not everyone is up to the challenge of living with one. By the same token, such a dog is easily marketed and thus easily exploited in breeding programs that seek profit over quality and proper placement.

Thus, it is to the benefit of American Eskimos, and their caretakers alike, for pet owners to leave breeding and showing to those compelled to pursue those passions in a quest to constantly improve the breed. The Eskie-owning family is wise to concentrate instead on the breed's heritage. Cherish this dog for what it offers as pet, companion and family member, and enjoy its qualities that have for so long endeared its kind to our species. If you view the dog in this light, you will find yourself the recipient of a special brand of canine loyalty that can only be appreciated fully by experience. Follow this tact and make your own contribution to the Eskie's illustrious history.

OFFICIAL STANDARD FOR THE AMERICAN ESKIMO DOG

General Appearance—The American Eskimo Dog, a loving companion dog, presents a picture of strength and agility, alertness and beauty. It is a small to medium-size Nordic type dog, nose, and eye rims). The white double coat consists of a short, dense undercoat, with a longer guard hair growing through it forming the outer coat, which is straight with no curl or wave. The

A solid white, agile and beautiful Nordic breed well describes the ideal American Eskimo Dog. The standard goes to great length to describe the Eskimo's coat, which must be prominent and impressive.

always white, or white with biscuit cream. The American Eskimo Dog is compactly built and well balanced, with good substance, and an alert, smooth gait. The face is Nordic type with erect triangular shaped ears, and distinctive black points (lips, coat is thicker and longer around the neck and chest forming a lion-like ruff, which is more noticeable on dogs than on bitches. The rump and hind legs down to the hocks are also covered with thicker, longer hair forming the characteristic breeches. The richly

Skull—Softly wedge-shaped.

Ears—Triangular, held erect.

Eyes—Slightly oval and set well apart

Ruff—Pronounced, more noticable in dogs than bitches.

Chest—Deep, broad, with well-sprung ribs.

Feet—oval, compact, and tightly knit.

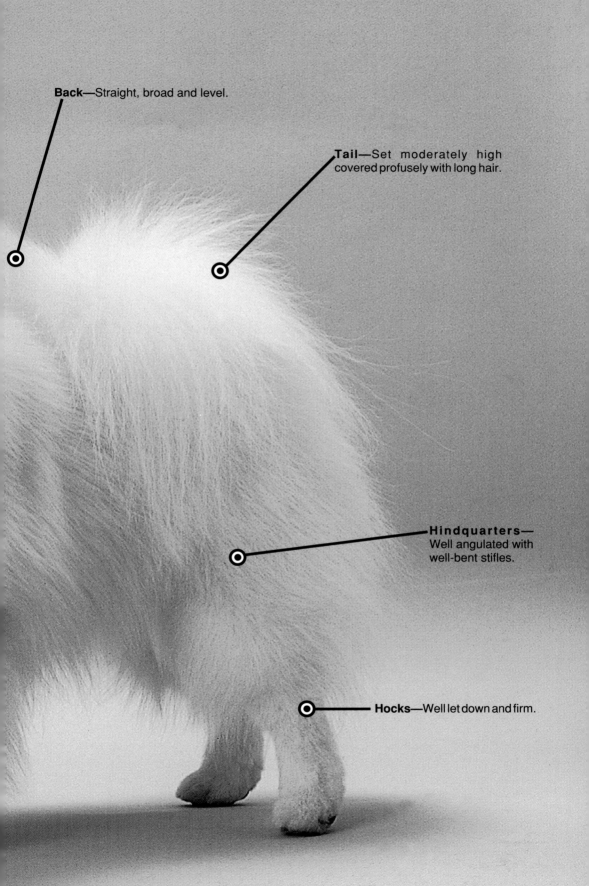

Back—Straight, broad and level.

Tail—Set moderately high covered profusely with long hair.

Hindquarters—Well angulated with well-bent stifles.

Hocks—Well let down and firm.

The expression of the American Eskimo is keen, intelligent and alert. This is a unique and personable companion dog whose sweet temperament must always shine through.

Head—*Expression* is keen, intelligent, and alert. *Eyes* are not fully round, but slightly oval. They should be set well apart, and not slanted, prominent or bulging. Tear stain, unless severe, is not to be faulted. Presence of tear stain should not outweigh consideration of type, structure, or temperament. Dark to medium brown is the preferred eye color. Eye rims are black to dark brown. Eyelashes are white. Faults: amber eye color or pink eye rims. *Disqualification: blue eyes. Ears* should conform to head size and be triangular, slightly blunt-tipped, held erect, set on high yet well apart, and blend softly with the head. *Skull* is slightly crowned and softly wedge-shaped, with widest breadth between the ears. The stop is well defined, although not abrupt. The muzzle is broad, with length not exceeding the length of the skull, although it may be slightly shorter. *Nose* pigment is black to dark brown. *Lips* are thin and tight, black to dark brown in color. Faults: pink nose pigment or pink lip pigment. The *jaw* should be strong with a full complement of close fitting teeth. The *bite* is scissors, or pincer.

plumed tail is carried loosely on the back.

Size, Proportion, Substance— *Size.* There are three separate size divisions of the American Eskimo Dog (all measurements are heights at withers): Toy, 9 inches to and including 12 inches; Miniature, over 12 inches to and including 15 inches; and Standard, over 15 inches to and including 19 inches. There is no preference for size within each division. *Disqualification: Under 9 inches or over 19 inches. Proportion.* Length of back from point of buttocks is slightly greater than height at withers, an approximate 1.1 to 1 ratio. *Substance.* The American Eskimo Dog is strong and compactly built with adequate bone.

Neck, Topline, Body—The *neck* is carried proudly erect, well set on, medium in length, and in a strong, graceful arch. The *topline* is level. The *body* of the American Eskimo Dog is strong and compact, but not cobby. The chest is deep and broad with well-sprung ribs. Depth of chest extends approximately to point of elbows. Slight tuck-up of belly just behind the ribs. The back is straight, broad, level, and muscular. The loin is strong and well muscled. The American Eskimo Dog is neither too long nor too short coupled. The *tail* is set moderately high and reaches approximately to the point of hock when down. It is carried loosely on the back, although it may be dropped when at rest.

shoulder the shoulder blade forms an approximate right angle with the upper arm. The legs are parallel and straight to the pasterns. The pasterns are strong and flexible with a slant of about 20°. Length of leg in proportion to the body. Dewclaws on the front legs may be removed at the owner's discretion; if present, they are not to be faulted. Feet are

Both the forequarters and hindquarters of the breed must be well angulated and in ideal proportion to the body.

Forequarters—Forequarters are well angulated. The shoulder is firmly set and has adequate muscle but is not over developed. The shoulder blades are well laid back and slant 45° with the horizontal. At the point of

oval, compact, tightly knit and well padded with hair. Toes are well arched. Pads are black to dark brown, tough and deeply cushioned. Toenails are white.

Hindquarters—Hindquarters are well angulated. The lay of the

Pure white defines the only color acceptable for the American Eskimo Dog, though some markings of biscuit or cream are permitted by the standard.

pelvis is approximately 30° to the horizontal. The upper thighs are well developed. Stifles are well bent. Hock joints are well let down and firm. The rear pasterns are straight. Legs are parallel from the rear and turn neither in nor out. Feet are as described for the front legs. Dewclaws are not present on the hind legs.

Coat—The American Eskimo Dog has a stand-off, double coat consisting of a dense undercoat and a longer coat of guard hair growing through it to form the outer coat. It is straight with no curl or wave. There is a pronounced ruff around the neck which is more noticeable on dogs than bitches. Outer part of the ear should be well covered with short, smooth hair, with longer tufts of hair growing in front of ear openings. Hair on muzzle should be short and smooth. The backs of the front legs should be well feathered, as are the rear legs down the hock. The tail is covered profusely with long hair. THERE IS TO BE NO TRIMMING OF THE WHISKERS OR BODY COAT AND SUCH TRIMMING WILL BE SEVERELY PENALIZED. The only permissible trimming is to neaten the feet and the backs of the rear pasterns.

Color— Pure white is the preferred color, although white with biscuit cream is permissible. Presence of biscuit cream should not outweigh consideration of type, structure, or temperament. The skin of the American Eskimo Dog is pink or gray. *Disqualification: any color other than white or biscuit cream.*

Gait—The American Eskimo Dog shall trot, not pace. The gait is agile, bold, well balanced, and frictionless, with good forequarter reach and good hindquarter drive. As speed increases, the American Eskimo Dog will single track with the legs converging toward the center line of gravity while the back remains firm, strong and level.

Temperament—The American Eskimo Dog is intelligent, alert, and friendly, although slightly conservative. It is never overly shy nor aggressive, and such dogs are to be severely penalized in the show ring. At home it is an excellent watchdog, sounding a warning bark to announce the arrival of any stranger. It is protective of its home and family, although it does not threaten to bite or attack people. The American Eskimo Dog learns new tasks quickly and is eager to please.

Disqualifications

Any color other than white or biscuit cream

Blue Eyes

Height: under 9" or over 19".

Approved: October 11, 1994
Effective: November 30, 1994

every litter of American Eskimos, type, structure and temperament must prevail, never allowing ~~any~~ other considerations to outweigh these breed essentials.

CHARACTERISTICS OF THE AMERICAN ESKIMO DOG

A rather perceptive, and very experienced, American Eskimo owner once made the observation that, "God made American Eskimos so beautiful so you wouldn't kill them."

On the surface this comment may sound mean-spirited, but it was coined by someone who adores the American Eskimo and whose ample experience with the breed inspired her to describe it in such a way that brings a grin of understanding to the faces of the countless others who share her passion. Live with an Eskie for even a short while, and you too will understand.

A GRAND OLD SOUL

While the appeal of the American Eskimo's beauty is universal, not every person is cut out to live with this dog. It does not stand as tall as many dogs, but its momentum is unstoppable, its spirit indomitable, its loyalty incorruptible. Now someone seeking a dog with the soft, compliant nature of say, the Golden Retriever, will probably not be happy in the company of a high-spirited, even domineering Eskie. It takes quite a bit of energy to live happily ever after with this white whirlwind, and only those properly prepared should take the plunge.

Don't be swayed by these fuzzy Eskie pups! These darlings inevitably grow into demanding and independent adults that need firm but fair training and leadership.

Unfortunately, far too many people fall in love with the absolutely adorable vision that is the American Eskimo puppy; a creature that both resembles and rivals the appearance of a polar bear cub. They soon learn as the dog matures, that this animal is far more than they bargained for. This accounts for the large number of Eskies that are relegated to the nation's animal shelters, having shed their soft white puppy fluff to make way for the lush double coat of the adult, and the intelligent, independent nature that comes with it.

Owners can do themselves and their dogs a favor by learning and internalizing the basic tenets of Eskie character. First, as we have said, this can be an incredibly domineering little animal. If its human family members fail to accept the leadership role in the household, the dog will gladly take that baton for itself. This, needless to say, is a recipe for disaster.

The American Eskimo requires discipline and leadership from a very young age, a fact that should not be translated to a commensurate need to strike or otherwise physically harm the animal to coerce him into doing his owner's bidding. Rather, an Eskie thrives best when handled according to the laws of positive reinforcement. He craves respect for his old soul and its savvy wit. Instead of punishing the dog when he doesn't behave or respond as you wish, set up situations in which he can succeed, and praise him profusely with words and treats for doing so.

Work with an American Eskimo in this way and you will be amazed at how quickly he learns, and how exuberantly he takes to his lessons. Whether teaching basic commands, playful tricks or the everyday routine of housebreaking, make the process

From the youngest age, Eskies absorb everything they see and hear, learning commands and tricks at alarming speeds. Involve your puppy in your daily activities and he will become biddable and mindful of your wishes.

a positive, exciting game and revel in the equally positive results you reap.

American Eskimos are legendary in the speed at which they learn. They tend to be the stars of their obedience classes, often leaping ahead in their lessons and even making up their own tricks along the way. The Eskie thrives best when asked to participate in his family's every activity, whether it be an obedience class, house cleaning or a construction project. He simply must feel an important part of the clan.

In keeping with their desire for constant stimulation of their minds, Eskies are especially fond of games, particularly those that require some thinking.

Take hide and seek, for example. Ask the dog to stay, hide somewhere in the house and call the dog to come looking for you. How it will rejoice when it finds you hiding behind a door! This author's own Eskie enjoys this and many games. He once decided after two catches of a Frisbee™ in his mouth that he preferred catching it in his two front paws like his owner did. He also taught himself to play football. After retrieving a small football thrown for him to fetch, he runs toward the defensive line formed by his owner. If he makes it through the line, he runs a short distance more and stops for the cheers that follow his touchdown. However, he has yet to learn how to spike the ball.

But despite this almost phenomenal intellect, don't overestimate this dog. It is a wise old soul that harbors a remarkably quick intelligence, but, if you come home to find it has torn apart the books you left on the floor or has urinated on the carpet, don't assume that your scoldings will have any meaning in regard to an action the dog perpetrated hours, or even minutes, before. Immediacy is the key, so if you don't catch the dog in the act, don't bother scolding. Instead, wait for a situation in which you can praise the dog, perhaps for staying away

American Eskimos need entertainment. Like any other highly intelligent breed, these dogs need to be occupied and supervised. Never trust an Eskie off-lead, no matter how well trained he is.

The "call of the wild" is too tempting for any Spitz dog, and the American Eskimo is no exception! The breed responds to its primitive instincts vocally and on its twos!

Originally a guardian of his family and home, the American Eskimo today takes his job as protector quite seriously. Don't encourage excessive barking or you'll never hear the end of it!

Eskimo's character. That incorruptible protective spirit is alive and well in the contemporary Eskie, and should be taken seriously by his owners.

The intensity of the Eskie's compulsion to protect can be softened by pursuing a structured socialization program beginning when the puppy is only a few weeks old. Introduce it to as many people outside of its own family as possible, as well as to other dogs. Enroll the pup in puppy kindergarten and then obedience class, and take him to visit friends and relatives and expose him to unfamiliar locales and situations whenever possible. Even introducing the Eskie to the experience of boarding at a young age should be part of this program, teaching the dog that staying temporarily at a kennel that is not its home with people

from the books and doing his business outdoors, keep him safely confined when you are not at home. This is a far more effective road toward progress.

Socialization is another area especially critical to the upbringing of the American Eskimo. This breed has quite a reputation for being not just wary, but downright nasty, toward strangers. Many a veterinarian and groomer has war stories, and often battle scars to match, of their experiences working with Eskies. This is a shame, really, as it is simply the result of improper socialization.

Travel back in this dog's history, back to a time when the Eskie's job was to guard his home, his family and his family's possessions, and that should be your first clue to the whys and wherefores of the American

Socializing the young pup can help the Eskie deal with his strong protective instincts.

who are not its owners need not be viewed as a threat. (By the same token, should the dog decide to dislike someone you have encountered, you are probably wise to heed this sensitive dog's opinion, not to mention its centuries-old sixth sense.)

Deliberate socialization of this kind will help convince the youngster—and ultimately the adult American Eskimo—that while it is acceptable for the dog to guard those it loves, it must not take this inclination to the extreme. This is all part of understanding and respecting, and living happily ever after with the unique soul that is the American Eskimo.

SUCCESSFUL PARTNERSHIPS

Indeed the overriding goal toward successful Eskie ownership is to understand how this dog's mind works and to work with it accordingly. The dog will readily offer its contributions toward its owners' education in this area. The owners just have to make the effort to listen.

If for example, today's Eskie enjoys barking and is ever ready to announce the arrival of someone at the door, it is not behaving in this way to annoy you and the neighbors. Rather, it is only doing what comes naturally to it. Nor should we be surprised at its profound need to protect its home and family. For centuries that has been its calling.

Every Eskie puppy possesses a unique character colored by his inherited instincts. Owners must dedicate time to training and socializing the American Eskimo to adapt to modern living.

American Eskimos make trustworthy mothers who often welcome the assistance of their human friends in the birthing and rearing process.

to help those who are arguing make amends by crawling into the laps of the perpetrators, by pleading with them to end the altercation or by playing the clown to get everyone laughing. More often than not, these efforts are successful. Who could possibly resist a dog behaving this way for the good of its family?

Not surprisingly, the Eskie is also a legendary lover of children. It has been known not only to defend children from would-be attackers and kidnappers, but even from parents who are attempting to discipline their offspring. As with any dog, however, young children should never be left alone with even the most trustworthy, affectionate Eskie. And all youngsters should be taught from a very young age to handle dogs with gentleness and respect.

If all within the family learn this lesson, life with an American Eskimo can be pure joy, filled with laughter and an unceasing sense of amazement at just how lively, how intelligent, how just plain fun this dog can be.

In this vein, the world is an oyster to the well-trained Eskie that has learned to behave and to adapt to any new experience thrown its way. Despite its independent spirit that keeps it analyzing and evaluating each and every situation, and individual it meets, the possibilities for fun for both the Eskie and its owners are endless. Eskies are, for example, great show dogs, but conformational showing requires dogs with

Living as it has for so many centuries in intimate proximity to its human families, the American Eskimo is extremely sensitive to the pack order of its family and to the interactions between the pack's members. While it may learn to tolerate and even lavish affection from strangers it meets in its daily life, it will choose a group of special individuals— usually a combination of immediate family members and friends—as its inner circle. These individuals are its pack.

The Eskie cannot abide disharmony among those it loves within its inner circle. In the event of an argument, it may react by leaving the room or by attempting certain physical attributes with which not every pet Eskie is blessed. Yet there are still a variety of other activities open to this dog that it and its owners may be even more pleased to pursue.

The American Eskimo's innate desire to perform makes it an ideal candidate for agility and obedience trials, activities open to any Eskie with the proper training and conditioning. The same holds true for work as therapy and hearing dogs. Many Eskies have enjoyed distinguished careers in these areas as well.

As long as it has a job to do, whether it be assisting in carrying laundry through the house to the laundry room, guarding the newly purchased stereo in the car, strutting its stuff in the obedience show ring or comforting a sick child in the hospital, the American Eskimo is ever ready to jump in and be a part of the action. He therefore requires an owner who will afford him ample opportunity to do so.

This well-balanced Eskie maneuvers himself on the seesaw obstacle at an agility trial. His patient owner and handler expectantly looks on.

YOUR NEW AMERICAN ESKIMO PUPPY

SELECTION

When you do pick out an American Eskimo puppy as a pet, don't be hasty; the longer you study puppies, the better you will understand them. Make it your transcendent concern to select only one that radiates good health and spirit and is lively on his feet, whose eyes are bright, whose coat

your arm or jacket appealing to your protective instinct. *Pick the American Eskimo puppy who forthrightly picks you! The feeling of attraction should be mutual!*

DOCUMENTS

Now, a little paper work is in order. When you purchase a purebred American Eskimo

Are you ready for an American Eskimo puppy to move into your life?! Look for a lively Eskie that is spirited in mind and body.

shines, and who comes forward eagerly to make and to cultivate your acquaintance. Don't fall for any shy little darling that wants to retreat to his bed or his box, or plays coy behind other puppies or people, or hides his head under

puppy, you should receive a transfer of ownership, registration material, and other "papers" (a list of the immunization shots, if any, the puppy may have been given; a note on whether or not the puppy has been wormed; a diet and

Puppy-proof your home before your Eskie steps through the front door. Before the exciting arrival of your pup, consider all the possible dangers in your home and decide where the puppy will be allowed to roam.

This beautiful American Eskimo puppy seems like he could fit into any home! Approach with caution: these snowwhite darlings can grow up to be truly "abominable" without proper training.

Eskimo puppies require considerable socialization and training. Your new furry charge depends on you for guidance and support.

Eskimos and puppies. True, you will run into many conflicting opinions, but at least you will not be starting "blind." Read, study, digest. Talk over your plans with your veterinarian, other "American Eskimo people," and the seller of your American Eskimo puppy.

When you get your American Eskimo puppy, you will find that your reading and study are far from finished. You've just scratched the surface in your plan to provide the greatest possible comfort and health for your American Eskimo; and, by the same token, you do want to assure yourself of the greatest possible enjoyment of this wonderful creature. You must be ready for this puppy mentally as well as in the physical requirements.

TRANSPORTATION

If you take the puppy home by car, protect him from drafts, particularly in cold weather. Wrapped in a towel and carried in the arms or lap of a passenger, the American Eskimo puppy will usually make the trip without mishap. If the pup starts to drool and to squirm, stop the car for a few minutes. Have newspapers handy in case of car-sickness. A covered carton lined with newspapers provides protection for puppy and car, if you are driving alone. Avoid excitement and unnecessary handling of the puppy on arrival. An American Eskimo puppy is a very small "package" to be making a complete change of surroundings

feeding schedule to which the puppy is accustomed) and you are welcomed as a fellow owner to a long, pleasant association with a most lovable pet, and more (news)paper work.

GENERAL PREPARATION

You have chosen to own a particular American Eskimo puppy. You have chosen it very carefully over all other breeds and all other puppies. So before you ever get that American Eskimo puppy home, you will have prepared for its arrival by reading everything you can get your hands on having to do with the management of American and company, and he needs frequent rest and refreshment to renew his vitality.

THE FIRST DAY AND NIGHT

When your American Eskimo puppy arrives in your home, put him down on the floor and don't pick him up again, except when it is absolutely necessary. He is a dog, a real dog, and must not be lugged around like a rag doll. Handle him as little as possible, and permit no one to pick him up without his mother and littermates. Comfort him and reassure him, but don't console him. Don't give him the "oh-you-poor-itsy-bitsy-puppy" treatment. Be calm, friendly, and reassuring. Encourage him to walk around and sniff over his new home. If it's dark, put on the lights. Let him roam for a few minutes while you and everyone else concerned sit quietly or go about your routine business. Let the puppy come back to you.

As tempting as cuddling your new Eskimo puppy is, give him time to explore his new surroundings and get comfortable. These three cuddly pups are ready for their new homes.

and baby him. To repeat, *put your American Eskimo puppy on the floor or the ground and let him stay there except when it may be necessary to do otherwise.*

Quite possibly your American Eskimo puppy will be afraid for a while in his new surroundings, Playmates may cause an immediate problem if the new American Eskimo puppy is to be greeted by children or other pets. If not, you can skip this subject. The natural affinity between puppies and children calls for some supervision until a live-and-let-live relationship is established. This applies particularly to a Christmas puppy, when there is more excitement than usual and more chance for a puppy to swallow something upsetting. It is a better plan to welcome the puppy several days before or after the holiday week. Like a baby, your American Eskimo puppy needs much rest and should not be over-handled. Once a child realizes that a puppy has "feelings" similar to his own, and can readily be hurt or injured, the opportunities for play and responsibilities provide exercise and training for both.

For his first night with you, he should be put where he is to sleep every night—say in the kitchen,

Your Eskimo will eventually be able to tell you when he wants to go out—and when he wants to come in!

since its floor can usually be easily cleaned. Let him explore the kitchen to his heart's content; close doors to confine him there. Prepare his food and feed him lightly the first night. Give him a pan with some water in it—not a lot, since most puppies will try to drink the whole pan dry. Give him an old coat or shirt to lie on. Since a coat or shirt will be strong in human scent, he will pick it out to lie on, thus furthering his feeling of security in the room where he has just been fed.

HOUSEBREAKING HELPS

Now, sooner or later—mostly sooner—your new American Eskimo puppy is going to "puddle" on the floor. First take a newspaper and lay it on the puddle until the urine is soaked up onto the paper. *Save this paper.* Now take a cloth with soap and water, wipe up the floor and dry it well. Then take the wet paper and place it on a fairly large square of newspapers in a convenient corner. When cleaning up, always keep a piece of wet paper on top of the others. Every time he wants to "squat," he will seek out this spot and use the papers. (This routine is rarely necessary for more than three days.) Now leave your American Eskimo puppy for the night. Quite probably he will cry and howl a bit; some are more stubborn than others on this matter. But let him stay alone for the night. This may seem harsh treatment, but it is the best procedure in the long run. Just let him cry; he will weary of it sooner or later.

FEEDING YOUR ESKIMO

Now let's talk about feeding your American Eskimo, a subject so simple that it's amazing there is so much nonsense and misunderstanding about it. Is it expensive to feed an American Eskimo? No, it is not! You can feed your American Eskimo economically and keep him in perfect shape the year round, or you can feed him expensively. He'll thrive either way, and let's see why this is true.

First of all, remember an American Eskimo is a dog. Dogs do not have a high degree of selectivity in their food, and unless you spoil them with great variety (and possibly turn them into poor, "picky" eaters) they will eat almost anything that they become accustomed to. Many dogs flatly refuse to eat nice, fresh beef. They pick around it and eat everything else. But meat—bah! Why? They aren't accustomed to it! They'd eat rabbit fast enough, but they refuse beef because they aren't used to it.

Choose a high-quality puppy chow for your new Eskimo puppy. Find out what the breeder has fed the pup previously and never change the pup's diet suddenly.

VARIETY NOT NECESSARY

A good general rule of thumb is forget all human preferences and don't give a thought to variety. Choose the right diet for your American Eskimo and feed it to him day after day, year after year, winter and summer. But what is the right diet?

Hundreds of thousands of dollars have been spent in canine nutrition research. The results are pretty conclusive, so you needn't go into a lot of experimenting with trials of this and that every other week. Research has proven just what your dog needs to eat and to keep healthy.

DOG FOOD

There are almost as many right diets as there are dog experts, but the basic diet most often recommended is one that consists of a dry food, either meal or kibble form. There are several of excellent quality, manufactured by reliable companies, research tested, and nationally advertised. They are inexpensive, highly satisfactory, and easily available in stores everywhere in containers of five to 50 pounds. Larger amounts cost less per pound, usually.

If you have a choice of brands, it is usually safer to choose the better known one; but even so, carefully read the analysis on the package. Do not choose any food in which the protein level is less than 25 percent, and be sure that this protein comes from both animal and vegetable sources. The good dog foods have meat meal, fish meal, liver, and such, plus protein from alfalfa and soy beans, as well as some dried-milk product. Note the vitamin content carefully. See that they are all there in good proportions; and be especially certain that the food contains properly high levels of vitamins A and D, two of the most perishable and important ones. Note the B-complex level, but don't worry about carbohydrate and mineral levels. These substances are plentiful and cheap and not likely to be lacking in a good brand.

The advice given for how to choose a dry food also applies to moist or canned types of dog foods, if you decide to feed one of these.

Carrots are rich in fiber, carbohydrates and vitamin A. The Carrot Bone™ by Nylabone® is a durable chew containing no plastics or artificial ingredients and it can be served as is, in bone hard form, or microwaved to a biscuity consistency.

Having chosen a really good food, feed it to your American Eskimo as the manufacturer directs. And once you've started, stick to it. Never change if you can possibly help it. A switch from one meal or kibble-type food can usually be made without too much upset; however, a change will almost invariably give you (and your American Eskimo) some trouble.

WHEN SUPPLEMENTS ARE NEEDED

Now what about supplements of various kinds, mineral and vitamin, or the various oils? They are all okay to add to your American Eskimo's food. However, if you are feeding your American Eskimo a correct diet, and this is easy to do, no supplements are necessary unless your American Eskimo has been improperly fed, has been sick, or is having puppies. Vitamins and minerals are naturally present in all the foods; and to ensure against any loss through processing, they are added in concentrated form to the dog food you use. Except on the advice of your veterinarian, added amounts of vitamins can prove harmful to your American Eskimo! The same risk goes with minerals.

FEEDING SCHEDULE

When and how much food to give your American Eskimo? Most dogs do better if fed two or three smaller meals per day—this is not only better but vital to larger and deep-chested dogs. As to how to prepare the food and how much to give, it is generally best to follow

Determine your American Eskimo's feeding schedule before the puppy can get his paw in the planning!

the directions on the food package. Your own American Eskimo may want a little more or a little less.

Fresh, cool water should always be available to your American Eskimo. This is important to good health throughout his lifetime.

ALL AMERICAN ESKIMOS NEED TO CHEW

Puppies and young American Eskimos need something with resistance to chew on while their teeth and jaws are developing—for cutting the puppy teeth, to induce growth of the permanent teeth under the puppy teeth, to assist in getting rid of the puppy teeth at the proper time, to help the permanent teeth through the gums, to ensure normal jaw

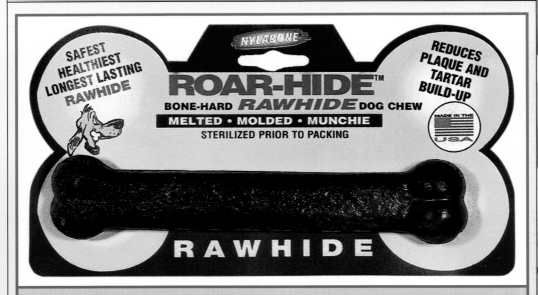

Roar-Hide™ by Nylabone® is completely edible and high in protein (over 86 percent) and very low in fat. Unlike common rawhide, it is safe, less messy, and more fun for your American Eskimo.

development, and to settle the permanent teeth solidly in the jaws.

The adult American Eskimo's desire to chew stems from the instinct for tooth cleaning, gum massage, and jaw exercise—plus the need for an outlet for periodic doggie tensions.

This is why dogs, especially puppies and young dogs, will often destroy property worth hundreds of dollars when their chewing instinct is not diverted from their owner's possessions. And this is why you should provide your American Eskimo with something to chew— something that has the necessary functional qualities, is desirable from the American Eskimo's viewpoint, and is safe for him.

It is very important that your American Eskimo not be permitted to chew on anything

he can break or on any indigestible thing from which he can bite sizable chunks. Sharp pieces, such as from a bone which can be broken by a dog, may pierce the intestinal wall and kill. Indigestible things that can be bitten off in chunks, such as from shoes or rubber or plastic toys, may cause an intestinal stoppage (if not regurgitated) and bring painful death, unless surgery is promptly performed.

Strong natural bones, such as 4- to 8-inch lengths of round shin bone from mature beef—either the kind you can get from a butcher or one of the variety available commercially in pet stores—may serve your American Eskimo's teething needs if his mouth is large enough to handle them effectively. You may be tempted to give your American Eskimo puppy

Since 1952, Tropical Fish Hobbyist has been the source of accurate, up-to-the-minute, and fascinating information on every facet of the aquarium hobby. Join the many thousands of devoted readers worldwide who wouldn't miss a single issue.

Subscribe right now so you don't miss a single copy!

Reptile Hobbyist is the source for accurate, up-to-the-minute, practical information on ever facet of the herpetological hobl **Join many thousand** of devoted readers worldwide who wouldn't miss a single valuable issu

Subscribe right now
so you don't miss a single copy!

a smaller bone and he may not be able to break it when you do, but puppies grow rapidly and the power of their jaws constantly increases until maturity. This means that a growing American Eskimo may break one of the smaller bones at any time, swallow the pieces, and die painfully before you realize what is wrong.

All hard natural bones are very abrasive. If your American Eskimo is an avid chewer, natural bones may wear away his teeth prematurely; hence, they then should be taken away from your dog when the teething purposes have been served. The badly worn, and usually painful, teeth of many mature dogs can be traced to excessive chewing on natural bones.

Contrary to popular belief, knuckle bones that can be chewed up and swallowed by your American Eskimo provide little, if any, usable calcium or other nutriment. They do, however, disturb the digestion of most dogs and cause them to vomit the nourishing food they need.

Dried rawhide products of various types, shapes, sizes, and prices are available on the market and have become quite popular. However, they don't serve the primary chewing functions very well; they are a bit messy when wet from mouthing, and most American Eskimos chew them up rather rapidly—but they have been considered safe for dogs until recently. Now, more and more incidents of death, and near death, by strangulation have been reported to be the results of partially swallowed chunks of rawhide swelling in the throat. More recently, some veterinarians have been attributing cases of acute constipation to large pieces of incompletely digested rawhide in the intestine.

A new product, molded rawhide, is very safe. During the process, the rawhide is melted and then injection molded into

Introduce puppies to chew toys at a young age. This baby Eskimo is sharpening his new teeth on a Chooz™ treat from Nylabone®.

Select only safe chew toys for your American Eskimo. Veterinarians and top breeders recommend Nylabone® products, which come in over 100 varieties, sizes and shapes. This is the Chicken N Cheese Pooch Pacifier™ from Nylabone®.

being longer lasting than other things offered for the purpose, they are economical.

Hard chewing raises little bristle-like projections on the surface of the nylon bones—to provide effective interim tooth cleaning and vigorous gum massage, much in the same way your toothbrush does it for you. The little projections are raked off and swallowed in the form of thin shavings, but the chemistry of the nylon is such that they break down in the stomach fluids and pass through without effect.

The toughness of the nylon provides the strong chewing resistance needed for important jaw exercise and effectively aids teething functions, but there is no tooth wear because nylon is non-abrasive. Being inert, nylon does not support the growth of microorganisms; and it can be washed in soap and water or it can be sterilized by boiling or in an autoclave.

the familiar dog shape. It is very hard and is eagerly accepted by American Eskimos. The melting process also sterilizes the rawhide. Don't confuse this with pressed rawhide, which is nothing more than small strips of rawhide squeezed together.

The nylon bones, especially those with natural meat and bone fractions added, are probably the most complete, safe, and economical answer to the chewing need. Dogs cannot break them or bite off sizable chunks; hence, they are completely safe—and

Pet shops sell treats that are healthy and nutritious. Cheese is added to chicken meal, rawhide and other high-protein foods to be melted together and molded into hard chew devices. Don't waste your money on low-protein treats. If the protein content isn't at least 50%, pass it up!

Nylabone® is highly recommended by veterinarians as a safe, healthy nylon bone that can't splinter or chip. Nylabone® is frizzled by the dog's chewing action, creating a toothbrush-like surface that cleanses the teeth and massages the gums. Nylabone® is superior to the cheaper bones because it is made of virgin nylon, which is the strongest and longest-lasting type of nylon available. The cheaper bones are made from recycled or re-ground nylon scraps, and have a tendency to break apart and split easily.

Nothing, however, substitutes for periodic professional attention for your American Eskimo's teeth and gums, not any more than your toothbrush can do that for you. Have your American Eskimo's teeth cleaned at least once a year by your veterinarian (twice a year is better) and he will be happier, healthier, and far more pleasant to live with.

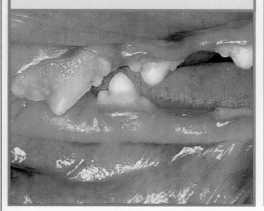

ABOVE: From a scientific study, this photograph shows a dog's tooth while being maintained by Gumabone® chewing.
BELOW: The Gumabone® chewing device was taken away and in 30 days the tooth was almost completely covered with tartar and plaque.

Once your American Eskimo has frayed both sides of the Nylabone®, it's time to replace it with a new one. Nylabone/Gumabone® Pooch Pacifiers enable the Eskimo to slowly chew off the knobs while they clean their own teeth. The knobs develop elastic frays that act like a toothbrush.

SHOWING YOUR AMERICAN ESKIMO

A show American Eskimo is a comparatively rare thing. He is one out of several litters of puppies. He happens to be born with a degree of physical perfection that closely approximates the standard by which the breed is judged in the show ring. Such a dog should, on maturity, be able to win or approach his championship in good, fast company at the larger shows. Upon finishing his championship, he is apt to be as highly desirable as a breeding animal. As a proven stud, he will automatically command a high price for service.

Showing American Eskimos is a lot of fun—yes, but it is a highly competitive sport. While all the experts were once beginners, the odds are against a novice. You will be showing against experienced handlers, often people who have devoted a lifetime to breeding,

This is Champion Frostiwyt Staker Bootnick, the first American Eskimo Dog Best of Breed at the Westminster Kennel Club (1996). He is owned by Carolyn E. Jester and bred by Nathan and Denise Staker.

picking the right ones, and then showing those dogs through to their championships. Moreover, the most perfect American Eskimo ever born has faults, and in your hands the faults will be far more evident than with the experienced handler who knows how to minimize his American Eskimo's faults. These are but a few points on the sad side of the picture.

The experienced handler, as I say, was not born knowing the ropes. He learned—*and so can you!* You can if you will put in the same time, study and keen observation that he did. But it will take time!

KEY TO SUCCESS

First, search for a truly fine show prospect. Take the puppy home, raise him by the book, and as carefully as you know how, give him every chance to mature

Chana, owned by Terri Pinney, showing off her first place agility ribbon.

A multiple high score winner, this is U-CD Grand Champion "PR" Aqua Mist Royal Echo, amid some of her many trophies.

into the American Eskimo you hoped for. My advice is to keep your dog out of big shows, even Puppy Classes, until he is mature. Maturity in the male is roughly two years; with the female, 14 months or so. When your American Eskimo is approaching maturity, start out at match shows, and, with this experience for both of you, then go gunning for the big wins at the big shows.

Next step, read the standard by which the American Eskimo is judged. Study it until you know

it by heart. Having done this, and while your puppy is at home (where he should be) growing into a normal, healthy American Eskimo, go to every dog show you can possibly reach. Sit at the ringside and watch American Eskimo judging. Keep your ears and eyes open. Do your own judging, holding each of those dogs against the standard, which you now know by heart.

In your evaluations, don't start looking for faults. Look for the virtues—the best qualities. How does a given American Eskimo shape up against the standard? Having looked for and noted the virtues, then note the faults and see what prevents a given American Eskimo from standing correctly or moving well. Weigh these faults against the virtues, since, ideally, every feature of the dog should contribute to the harmonious whole dog.

"RINGSIDE JUDGING"

It's a good practice to make notes on each American Eskimo,

Champion "PR" Steven's Snow Princess, owned by Rosemary Stevens.

always holding the dog against the standard. In "ringside judging," forget your personal preference for this or that feature. What does the standard say about it? Watch carefully as the judge places the dogs in a given class. It is difficult from the ringside always to see why number one was placed over the second dog. Try to follow the judge's reasoning. Later try to talk with the judge after he is finished. Ask him questions as to why he placed certain American Eskimos and not others. Listen while the judge explains his placings, and, I'll say right here, any judge worthy of his license should be able to give reasons.

When you're not at the ringside, talk with the fanciers and breeders who have American Eskimos. Don't be afraid to ask opinions or say that you don't know. You have a lot of listening to do, and it will help you a great deal and speed up your personal progress if you are a good listener.

U-CD Grand Champion "PR" Sweetwater's Encore, TT has won many Bests in Show for owner-breeder Monica Sellers.

THE NATIONAL CLUB

You will find it worthwhile to join the national American Eskimo club and to subscribe to its magazine. From the national club, you will learn the location of an approved regional club near you. Now, when your young American Eskimo is eight to ten months old, find out the dates of match shows in your section of the country. These differ from regular shows only in that no championship points are given. These shows are especially designed to launch young dogs (and new handlers) on a show career.

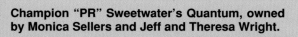

Champion "PR" Sweetwater's Quantum, owned by Monica Sellers and Jeff and Theresa Wright.

Even at the tender age of four weeks, American Eskimo pups have minds of their own. As any breeder will relay, begin teaching manners from the first day so that your new charge understands what will be expected of him.

ENTER MATCH SHOWS

With the ring deportment you have watched at big shows firmly in mind and practice, enter your American Eskimo in as many match shows as you can. When in the ring, you have two jobs. One is to see to it that your American Eskimo is always being seen to its best advantage. The other job is to keep your eye on the judge to see what he may want you to do next. Watch only the judge and your American Eskimo. Be quick and be alert; do exactly as the judge directs. Don't speak to him except to answer his questions. If he does something you don't like, don't say so. And don't irritate the judge (and everybody else) by constantly talking and fussing with your dog.

In moving about the ring, remember to keep clear of dogs beside you or in front of you. It is my advice to you *not* to show your American Eskimo in a regular point show until he is at least close to maturity and after both you and your dog have had time to perfect ring manners and poise in the match shows.

Begin training your Eskimo tike for the show ring from an early age. Match shows are an excellent way to introduce yourself and your American Eskimo to the world of showing dogs.

TRAINING YOUR ESKIMO

You owe proper training to your American Eskimo. The right and privilege of being trained is his birthright; and whether your American Eskimo is going to be a handsome, well-mannered housedog and companion, a show dog, or whatever possible use he may be put to, the basic training is always the same—all must start with basic obedience, or what might be called "manner training."

Your American Eskimo must come instantly when called and obey the "Sit" or "Down" command just as fast; he must walk quietly at "Heel," whether on or off lead. He must be mannerly and polite wherever he goes; he must be polite to strangers on the street and in stores. He must be mannerly in the presence of other dogs. He must not bark at children, cars, motorcycles, or other domestic animals. And he must be restrained from chasing cats. It is not a dog's inalienable right to chase cats, and he must be reprimanded for it.

The good manners and behavior of your new American Eskimo puppy rely entirely on your shoulders.

PROFESSIONAL TRAINING

How do you go about this training? Well, it's a very simple procedure, pretty well standardized by now. First, if you can afford the extra expense, you may send your American Eskimo to a professional trainer, where in 30 to 60 days he will learn how to be a "good dog." If you enlist the services of a good professional trainer, follow his advice of when to come to see the dog. No, he won't forget you, but too-frequent visits at the wrong time may slow down his training progress. And using a "pro" trainer means that you will have

Basic obedience commands belong in the repertory of every companion dog. This American Eskimo is working beautifully with his young trainer.

There is such a group in nearly every community nowadays. Here you will be working with a group of people who are also just starting out. You will actually be training your own dog, since all work is done under the direction of a head trainer who will make suggestions to you and also tell you when and how to correct your American Eskimo's errors. Then, too, working with such a group, your American Eskimo will learn to get along with other dogs. And, what is more important, he will learn to do exactly what he is told to do, no matter how much confusion there is around him or how great the temptation is to go his own way.

One method of teaching the "Down" is by pulling the dog's front legs forward while saying the command "Down."

to go for some training, too, after the trainer feels your American Eskimo is ready to go home. You will have to learn how your American Eskimo works, just what to expect of him and how to use what the dog has learned after he is home.

OBEDIENCE TRAINING CLASS

Another way to train your American Eskimo (many experienced American Eskimo people think this is the best) is to join an obedience training class right in your own community.

Write to your national kennel club for the location of a training club or class in your locality. Sign up. Go to it regularly—every session! Go early and leave late! Both you and your American Eskimo will benefit tremendously.

TRAIN HIM BY THE BOOK

The third way of training your American Eskimo is by the book. Yes, you can do it this way and do a good job of it too. But in using the book method, select a book, buy it, study it carefully; then study it some more, until the procedures are almost second nature to you. Then start your training. But stay with the book and its advice and exercises. Don't start in and then make up a few rules of your own. If you don't follow the book, you'll get into jams you can't get out of by yourself. If after a few hours of short training sessions your American Eskimo is still not working as he should, get back to the book for a study session, because it's your fault, not the dog's! The procedures of dog training have been so well systemized that it must be your fault, since literally thousands of fine American Eskimos have been trained by the book.

Most trainers encourage the use of food rewards in training. Although certain breeds may respond to commands alone, the American Eskimo is best when motivated by a reward.

After your American Eskimo is "letter perfect" under all conditions, then, if you wish, go on to advanced training and trick work. Your American Eskimo will love his obedience training, and you'll burst with pride at the finished product! Your American Eskimo will enjoy life even more, and you'll enjoy your American Eskimo more. And remember— you *owe good training to your American Eskimo.*

YOUR HEALTHY AMERICAN ESKIMO DOG

The American Eskimo is a breed of many blessings, one of these being its relatively good health. Eskies are long lived, prone to few serious health problems, and should live well into their teens with a lust for life that makes those it meets believe the elderly Eskie must surely be a puppy. This natural vitality relies,

THE DOG BEAUTIFUL

Long ago, the Eskie was christened "the dog beautiful." One look at this animal and there is little doubt why. Downright disarming in its white splendor, the healthy Eskie can't help but command attention from an adoring public as it trots down the street with its owner in tow,

In good health, the American Eskimo retains its youthful vigor and beauty until its teen years. Sound maintenance, nutrition and veterinary assistance help realize this goal for every owner.

however, on the willingness of the dog's owner to assist his or her pet, through both grooming and health maintenance, in fulfilling its healthy destiny.

its eyes sparkling with mischief, its coat shimmering in the sun.

But what the public may find surprising is just how natural that Eskie beauty is. In her

Mischief mingled with convincing innocence: the expression of the Eskimo puppy is unmistakably its own.

Brushing is key to keeping the Eskimo's coat clean and white. Accustoming the young dog to relaxing during the brushing sessions greatly simplifies this bi-daily chore.

infinite wisdom, Mother Nature has graced the American Eskimo with a lovely double coat—a soft fluffy undercoat protected by longer, coarser guard hairs that shield the insulating undercoat and the skin from the elements. This coat, an engineering miracle, not only regulates the dog's body temperature, but also seems to miraculously clean itself.

Many a fledgling Eskie puppy owner has blanched when his or her pup has romped in the mud that first time, only to discover an hour later that all the dirt has simply fallen away, leaving the pup with the same white puppy fluff it had before its muddy adventure. So while we may assume a dog of this stunning white coat would need frequent

Although show dogs are bathed every week before the big event, pet American Eskimos will not need to be bathed as frequently. Whenever your Eskie has muddied himself up, a bath is likely your best resort.

bathing, a bath every two or three months is usually all the animal requires (unless of course it is suffering from fleas or is a busy show dog, both of which are situations that may call for more frequent, even weekly, bathing).

This is not to say that you may simply ignore the Eskie's grooming needs, however. While indeed this dog may be somewhat obsessed with cleanliness, prone to cleaning itself like a cat, it, like any dog, requires routine grooming, which is best introduced to the dog in a positive light when as a young puppy.

The most important element to keeping the Eskie beautiful, is brushing. Take a pin or slicker brush to the dog every week (or preferably every other day or so)

Keep your Eskimo's nails trim. Use a nail clipper available from your pet-supply store, and proceed with caution. Never clip too deeply into the nail or it will bleed. If you're gentle and careful, your Eskimo will cooperate (usually!).

Don't ignore the Eskimo's teeth in your grooming regimen. A doggy toothbrush and paste (such as 2-Brush™ by Nylabone®) are available at your pet-supply store.

to keep his coat healthy, lustrous, and free of mats and dead hair. Make sure to brush all the way down to the skin, and pay close attention to the ruff, the area behind the ears and the hindquarters, all of which can be prone to matting. Don't be shocked if twice a year the dog's undercoat begins to come out in clumps. This is natural for double-coated dogs, known as "blowing the coat," and requires daily brushing until the coat is completely blown.

Complete the grooming regimen by trimming the dog's nails on a regular basis (clip only the tips and avoid the darker, blood-rich quick which will bleed profusely if nicked), and pay attention to the ears. You may clean the ear flaps with mineral oil and a cotton ball (never place anything inside the ear), and smell the ears regularly to make sure they do not develop

After a romp in the back yard, check your Eskimo for possible parasites—especially in the warm months.

a strange odor that could indicate an infection. Top this off with regular, preferably daily, toothbrushing (supplemented by annual or twice-annual cleanings by the veterinarian), and your pup should have no trouble living up to its reputation as the "dog beautiful."

If you've selected your new Eskimo wisely, the pup will already have seen a veterinarian. Breeders bring their whole litters to the vet for routine examination and inoculations before potential buyers ever see them.

PREVENTION AS MEDICINE

Just as attention to the American Eskimo's minimal grooming needs will help the dog lead a healthy, contented existence, so will adherence to a program of sound preventive medicine. This must be pursued in partnership with the dog's veterinarian. The doctor will provide those professional medical services necessary to keep the dog healthy, and he or she will in turn rely on the owner to remain on the lookout for signs that could indicate a budding health problem that is best combated with early treatment.

Your American Eskimo will be ever grateful for the time and money you put into its good health—an investment that will return for you tenfold!

Take your new Eskimo to the veterinarian right away—do not wait a week or a month. You cannot risk bringing a sickly animal into your home. You cannot afford the financial hardship or the heartbreak that follows.

The major components to the Eskie's—or any dog's—preventive health care, are its vaccines. These begin when the dog is a puppy, usually at around six weeks of age. At this time the youngster is vaccinated with a combination vaccine against parvovirus, coronavirus, leptospirosis, distemper and infectious hepatitis. This must then be repeated every few weeks until the pup has received a series of three or four vaccines and has reached at least 16 weeks of age (many vets today are recommending an additional parvovirus vaccine at five or six months to ensure full protection). The initial series should then be followed by a booster every year thereafter. The rabies vaccine is administered when the pup reaches four months of age,

followed by boosters every one or three years. An appointment for annual boosters provides the ideal opportunity for the dog's annual checkup with the veterinarian, an event that may become twice yearly as the dog ages.

Parasite control is another important ingredient in the prevention plan. Controlling fleas, for example, will not only make the dog more comfortable, but also help prevent an internal infestation of tapeworms, which are carried by fleas. In pursuing this potentially frustrating endeavor, make sure to treat the dog, his bed, your home and the yard immediately, during flea season as well as on a regular basis. Treating only the dog will

Likely your new Eskimo will be as healthy and vibrant as this young dog. Trust your veterinarian to establish an inoculation and general check-up schedule.

Your American Eskimo should be kept from direct sunlight. Heatstroke commonly kills dogs left in the direct sun, especially heavily coated dogs. Direct sun can also damage the Eskimo's beautiful coat.

not suffice, as the flea life cycle involves the dog as well as its environment, so you will up the odds of success by targeting all fronts and using products as directed.

You should also have your pet's feces examined twice a year by the veterinarian to ensure the dog has not been invaded by any of the internal parasites that target canine hosts. Most of these are quite benign, but beware of the heartworm. Carried by mosquitoes, this lethal parasite of the heart can kill a dog and prove difficult if not impossible to eradicate. Fortunately it may be prevented with a monthly medication available by prescription from a veterinarian.

Another important step toward keeping the Eskie as healthy as

Typical of the breed, the Eskimo places his complete trust in his owner.

Brushing with a pinbrush every other day is the basis for your American Eskimo's grooming routine. Whenever brushing your dog, keep an eye out for parasites or other signs of problems.

The altered pet is also a better pet in that, free of the callings of those powerful hormonal urges, it is more interested in spending time with its family than in pursuing liaisons with others of its own kind. It is best to ignore the myths that altered dogs are fat or lazy. While one rarely sees an overweight Eskie, whether altered or intact, *all* dogs require exercise, and an active, properly exercised dog on a healthy, well-balanced diet will not be overweight.

THE ATTENTIVE OWNER

Unfortunately, no matter how careful we are in fostering our

As trainer, provider and companion, you are your Eskimo's best friend.

possible is having the dog spayed or neutered. While an altered dog will not contribute to the heartbreaking problem of pet overpopulation, as an added bonus, it will probably live a healthier, longer life, and probably be a better, more attentive pet, as well.

Ideally, the Eskie pup should be spayed or neutered before or when it reaches six months of age. Research has shown that the earlier a dog is altered, the less risk it has of developing severe reproduction-related ailments such as mammary cancer, testicular cancer, and the various disorders and infections that plague the reproductive organs.

Invest in a grooming table for your American Eskimo. Since you will be brushing your dog three or four times a week, this purchase pays off by making the sessions quicker and easier (and saving you any stress on your back and knees).

An active, intelligent breed like the American Eskimo Dog needs plenty of outdoor time to run off its energy. Like other Nordic dogs, American Eskimos are gregarious with other members of their breed.

It pays for an owner to know his American Eskimo. More than anyone else, you will know when your puppy or dog is not feeling his best. Be attentive—your Eskie is counting on you.

dogs' health and well-being, even the healthiest pet may succumb to illness and/or injury at one time or another. The observant owner will notice instantly if the dog suddenly stops eating, vomits, has diarrhea, becomes lethargic and depressed, develops unusual lumps or bumps on its skin, walks with a humped back, or drinks and urinates excessively, all of which are the classic signs of canine illness that should be reported to the veterinarian as soon as possible.

In taking such symptoms seriously, the attentive owner can either prevent the onset of serious illness, or help to ensure that such a condition is caught and treated in its earliest stages—

perhaps saving the dog's life. The benefit of living with American Eskimos is that these dogs are so involved with their families, and so lively in their pursuit of fun and daily adventure, that even the slightest change in behavior or demeanor becomes a neon light to the owner who is paying attention.

The properly cared for Eskie should get through life with little trouble. Although this may change with the Eskie's increasing popularity that too often leads to indiscriminate breeding, the breed is not presently known for high incidences of relatively common genetic conditions, such as hip dysplasia (a deformity of the hip joint) or various eye maladies that are passed on from parent to puppy. But, they are not immune to the troubles that can affect any dog, and the owner of even the healthiest Eskie should remain on alert for the signs.

Canine bloat, for instance, is not common in Eskies, but if you notice that your pet appears to be in pain and exhibits a swollen abdomen following a meal, especially after a meal it has wolfed down after a vigorous exercise session, get the dog to the veterinarian immediately as it may be suffering from this life-threatening condition.

Heatstroke is another condition that can strike the unsuspecting American Eskimo, especially

Tooth decay is common in all breeds of dog. Your veterinarian will examine your Eskimo's teeth regularly. Providing quality safe chew toys (such as Nylabone® and Gumabone®) can save your dog's teeth.

If your American Eskimos are kept outdoors during the daytime, be sure that there is plenty of water and shade. You must guard against heatstroke for your dogs by providing appropriate accommodations and avoiding rigorous exercise on hot, humid days.

Pet shops sell biscuits for dogs that are nutritious and tasty. Read the label before you purchase doggy treats for your Eskimo. Avoid artificial ingredients and any additives that may be harmful to your dog.

when this thick-coated Nordic breed is subjected to vigorous exercise during the high heat of a sweltering summer day. Frantic panting, a staggering gait, excessive salivation and vomiting are all signs of heatstroke in dogs, and if the situation is not treated swiftly, the animal will lapse into a coma and die. Prevent heatstroke by reserving exercise for the cooler hours of the day, ensuring the dog has constant access to shade and cool water, and by leaving the dog home on even a mildly warm day, since confining it in a car even with the windows down can lead to heatstroke within minutes.

As they age, dogs become more prone to urinary tract disorders,

The dog's body temperature is a measuring device for possible infection. Your Eskimo's normal body temperature is 101.5º F (though the Toy variety and some Miniatures may be as high as 102º F).

As your American Eskimo ages, you will have to become more conscious of possible problems related to aging in dogs. Although he may retain much of his youthful vigor, his body will be slowing down.

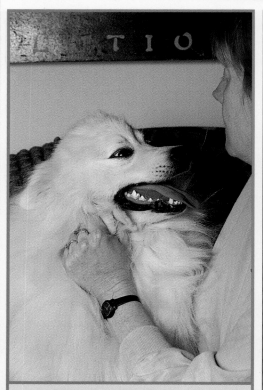

No matter how responsibly we care for our pets, we inevitably will outlive them. Make every day and every year in your American Eskimo's life count.

symptoms, and by knowing what to do in the event of illness, injury and emergency. If you enjoy hiking with your Eskie, for example (Eskies adore hiking), make sure you bring a canine first-aid kit along. When you return home, check the animal from head to toe to make sure it has not been cut or brought home a tick or embedded foxtail between its toes. Always keep the veterinarian's phone number, as well as the number of your local poison control center near the phone.

Despite swift responses to health situations, or one's allegiance to a sound preventive medicine program, we are inevitably fated to outlive our pets, and the day will come when

Maintaining the American Eskimo adult is a fairly simple matter. Be aware of the potential dangers in your dog's environment and be ready to handle them. Simple first aid and preventative care can make all the difference in your Eskie's life.

the signs for which owners are also in a position to monitor. If a dog has difficulty urinating, suddenly begins drinking more water than it ever has before, and urinates more frequently, or if you notice blood in the urine, something is amiss with the urinary tract that requires veterinary attention. The cause may be kidney disease or problems with the bladder, either of which can only be diagnosed and treated by a veterinarian.

It is best to be prepared where health is concerned, both by arming oneself with basic knowledge of canine illness and you will need to bid your dear one good-bye. This may come on the day when the dog quietly passes on in its sleep or succumbs naturally to an illness, or it may come about when you must make the decision to have it humanely put to sleep due to a severe injury or illness with which it simply isn't fair to ask the animal to suffer.

Regardless of the nature of a dog's end, saying good-bye is never easy. You are bidding farewell to a family member, in the case of the American Eskimo, a family member that has refused to allow any activity to proceed without its participation. It is best when that time comes, to reflect on those many wonderful memories, and be thankful that you had the privilege of sharing life with this special creature. Later, after you have healed some, don't be surprised if you find you simply must take another of these delightful dogs into your home and family. Most find that once they have lived with the American Eskimo, the experience is permanently addictive.

ying good-bye to a beloved pet is never easy. Remember the good times, the funny puppy moments, e adorable adult moments: soon a new baby Eskimo will be clamoring for your love and affection.

SUGGESTED READING

TS-214
432 pages
over 300 full-color photos.

TS-205
160 pages
130 full-color photos.

TS-258
160 pages
over 200 full-color photos.

TS-257
384 pages
Over 800 full-color photos.